The Hope of the Air

The Hope of the Air

poems by

Barry Spacks

Michigan State University Press
East Lansing

Michigan State University Press
East Lansing, Michigan 48823-5245

Printed and bound in the United States of America.

10 09 08 07 06 05 04 1 2 3 4 5 6 7 8 9 10

LIBRARY OF CONGRESS CATALOGING-IN-PUBLICATION DATA
Spacks, Barry.
The hope of the air: poems / by Barry Spacks.
p.   cm.
ISBN 0-87013-732-8 (pbk.: alk. paper)
1. Title.
PS3569.P33H67 2004
811'.54–dc22
2004012347

Michigan State University Press is a member of the Green Press Initiative and is
committed to developing and encouraging ecologically responsible publishing practices.
For more information about the Green Press Initiative and the use of recycled paper in
book publishing, please visit www.greenpressinitiative.org.

Book and cover design by Valerie Brewster, Scribe Typography
Cover photo is by Kimberley Snow and is used courtesy of the photographer.

Visit Michigan State University Press on the World Wide Web at:

www.msupress.msu.edu

for Dan Gerber

guide, philosopher, and friend

Contents

PART ONE

PART TWO

PART THREE

The Hope of the Air

Part One

Metaphysics at the Beach

We said mere facts were the mind's maneuver:
made up – though a touch of the so-called 'real'
might serve to spin a vision on,
as a pearl takes a grain of sand for its start.

As if it had heard, at once the wind,
till then at rest invisibly,
stirred in a gust a storm of sand
salting our hair, pelting our skin,

billions of seeds
for the weaving of pearls:
wind's sense of humor:
"Here. For your fictions."

Actors' Exercise

First you're to march – later run – across stage:
toward the flats, the forklift in the wings,
some member of the cast assigned
to halt you with a cautioning hand
before you crash into prop or trashcan
blind. Will your guardian neglect you,
chatting? Well, you're to close your eyes
and imagine running straight through the wall.

You'll notice a strong desire to peep,
a certain slowing of pace toward the last,
a distinct conviction your Stopper's forgotten,
clowning, giggling, the saving task,
for the run seems endless. For timid faith,
for every pang of animal fear,
there's one adjustment: running faster.
Lovely. Again. Now try it backwards.

And now, out toward the footlights, the pit,
thinking, still blind, of your broken leg,
your battered head – to be brought to a stop
not by a hand or a tackle but solely
the one word "Halt" from the gathered cast
down in the dark theater. You halt,
one step from cliff-crash, to open your eyes
on whites and ambers, clapping and bravoes.

Fine. Surviving, you're ready to move,
eyes open, gliding like dancing Krishna
out of the shadows of shyness striding,
fluently you and deeply there,
seasoned past fear and every pinched gesture,

forgetting the Manners Police, swirling
your cape, doffing plumed hat. That's how
to prepare. Go on, have another bow.

The Assimilation

It's coming along, the assimilation,
though granted in certain parts of the world
like Idaho the pace seems slow
and nowhere exactly what you might call
a rush on skullcaps and circumcision;

but take my colleague Wayne O'Neil:
on the phone about some political mess
he calls it (three times) "this *mishegas!*"
plus the Jews on TV are heroes now,
charmers, played by Swedes, Italians,

so maybe – say in ten thousand years? –
discoursing Talmud, shrugging their shoulders,
even the grim ones will think to join us?
(we who take jokes as a serious business)
clapping, dancing, teasing in accents . . . .

Big Momma Bear

An old notion held that bear cubs were born shapeless,
and had to be licked into form.

FOOTNOTE TO LL. 101–2. BK. I, OF POPE'S *Dunciad*

A bear is born as a round fluffy bundle,
from which comes the saying "licked into shape"
as Momma Bear tongues up the bear-potential.

Who couldn't use Momma Bear re-creation?
We shake cold trees for what? a green apple?
Big Momma, grab us by the nape –

God knows you're rough – lurch back again
to that promising puddle of what we were
and lick yourself up some *bear.*

Oh, Everything, Absolute Giving!

When I was a kid working Saturdays
at the Quality Market, our family's market,
I'd toss back jokes at the butchers, open
brown paper bags with a whoosh, in charge
of cutting deals on wilted beans
graying grapefruit lining the floor
in green metal tins I bargained over
with the poor. One Christmas Eve,
inching my prices down out front
trying to sell the last of the wreathes,
the mistletoe and trees, all at once
without permission I shouted "Free!
Free Christmas stuff!" and could have thrown in
the fixtures, blood oranges, blood of the lamb,
such explosion of freedom, such joy filled me then,
handing out greens in Camden's hard cold.

Burst of Cumin

She'll laugh or she'll rage – no way to predict
who she'll be in a moment, or where.

She whispers and hairs at the back of my neck
rise up as if they were meant to hear.

She sighs, or turns steel, or she'll focus in
on one blossom so fully her gaze on its being

might make it think she's next-of-kin.
Her words are dark chocolate low-notes rising

to unheard vanillas . . . it's me who's gone
till she's here, but now I find her again

almost anywhere: in the peace of a stone;
a nudge of wind; a burst of cumin.

Aunts

Coming in from the cold in furs,
laughing, asking questions, teasing,
they teach a boy what he needs to know:
that looking in mirrors will freeze a face
to a single, fatuous expression;
that girls will envy curly hair;
that waltzing goes . . . one, two-three.

Aunts are always offering cake,
certain you couldn't have had enough.
How proudly they check you over, assessing
your readiness for a teenage date,
adjusting the set of a tie, saying
"Hold still, please.
Please, stand up straight!"

To a boy, Aunts are an Order of Angels,
the sort that gossip of humans, their voices
a subtle sweetness on the air.
There's something mildly scandalous,
you slim and grown, at a cousin's wedding,
something exciting and dangerous,
waltzing with your youngest Aunt.

Uncles

The world gets so sad without Uncles, natty
in summer in brown-and-white wingtip shoes,
shaving lotion, seersucker suits.
The furniture's draped with sheets, the family's

off to the seashore – an Uncle lifts you
out of the path of a monster wave;
he buys you a hotdog with slathers of mustard;
he lets you turn his steering wheel.

At Christmas, guided by one of the Uncles,
you go to *The Nutcracker,* wearing long-pants
(or your dress with the burgundy velvet ribbon
woven through the white) and once,

in a drama at school (attended by Uncles)
you played either *Bang* or *Crack* or *Pop,*
a Firecracker, shouting "Bang"
or "Crack" or "Pop," and Uncles applauded.

It may be in places even today,
since many are nieces and nephews forever,
the Uncles will still be arriving, with smiles,
with presents, in brown-and-white wingtip shoes.

The Death of Leonardo Vinci

No relation to Leonardo da
was Leonardo (non-da) Vinci,
post-Scarlatti, pre-Pergolesi,
composer of operas buffa and seria,
one "who would gamble his eyes away."

Listen, children: he died, poor as Mozart,
of so-called "colic," no time for confession,
on May 27th, 1730,
age thirty-four . . .
it seems that someone

poisoned your cocoa, poor Vinci, for bragging
of ease in seducing delicate women
in Rome: "her thoughts arched toward me . . . and then,
her body." Hard Romans managed such matters,
even at Naples, exactingly:

no second chance, once you'd understood,
as you choked, as you burned, why you'd been poisoned:
for shaming beauty – an artist, bringing
shame to beauty – Leonardo
(non-da) Vinci.

Dot

An image of the sun's great violence
flares full-page'd in a magazine,
sphere within molten sphere rotating
at varied speeds, like history,
yielding a non-stop Babel-broadcast,
a rage of tongues.

Below this orange-yellow-red explosion
our planet floats, proportionally
a dot: dark period: tiny bottom
of an exclamation point we live on!
And when our star implodes
the dot goes cold: dabbed White-Out.

I think of one among the Dotlings
who brings the miniature and vast together.
Jupiter itself might seem to him
no farther than a dewdrop on his shoulder.
He leaves his evening meditation
concerned with sadness in a troubled student,

a heavy mood of youth upon her,
and wonders if some skillful means of his
might help or hinder
as loud voices from the sun pour forth
through the redolence of emptiness
toward his calm and measured breathing.

Bachelard on Art

Composed of freely rearranged phrases from
Gaston Bachelard's *The Right to Dream,* a
posthumous collection of the philosopher
prefaces and introductions

We are really very ancient plants,
caught up in a dream of sonority;

immense charity toward the beautiful;

colors of the days of Paradise,

this Paradise that sings
before it speaks.

༕

Matter exists: stone slate wood copper.
Paper too, with its grain, its fiber.
Paper roused
from its nightmare of whiteness.

༕

The will to art: strange tissue
of patience and enthusiasm.
Hard materials; a world in labor.
Constant pains.
Induced surprises.

༕

A woman feels looked at
by the emerald's gentle eye.

The man who likes describing things
thinks things are glad to be seen.

The bottle
fills itself up.

The ink begins
to write its own poems.

Everything that shines
sees.

A House in Montecito

The white and blue villa
where the art professor lives
would be easier to take,
its plaque by Della Robia
on the outside white wall,

its pane of blue glass
that sends a pale blue light
across the sitting room, done
in Greek blues against the white,

if only he were sitting the house,
caring for the cats,
high-eared, long-legged out of Egypt,
for some absent owner Fat Cats
wintering in the islands.

But no, the cats and all are his,
the whole dear oasis,
so it's a son-of-a-bitch
to think of something right to say

about how lush it is, his zone of sea
that yields a special azure glow
just here and just for him
through colonnades
of sunstruck whiteness.

Buddha Songs

To gaze into an empty room
is not becoming Buddha.

To feed a starving lion, Buddha
gave up one of his precious lives.

As a rabbit, as food,
he leapt in the fire.

We're paired to help,
like hands, like feet.

To gaze into an empty room
is not becoming Buddha.

❧

What's lovable about a hum?
Needlessness. It stops, or continues.

Our shadows lie
on a moving stream.

Beautiful . . . to be beautiful
is all we need to offer each other.

This my cat knows,
and my trees.

Creatures

IN THE PIGPEN

Dog frisking, milky cow,
and a .22 Specialist at the fence.
Pop, a tiny sound, a perfect
hole between the eyes of the pig
who spouts, staggers, plops on its side
as the pig next in line
swills the pulsing blood,
completely beyond opinions.

GULL

I try to feed the morning gulls;
one snatches my bread-bits however I aim them,
no larger than the others but much
more fierce in the dance of competition,
scurrying at them yellow-eyed
till they skitter, humbled by her charge . . .
a beauty, like a great ballerina;
a beauty despite – or because of – greed.

GRANDFATHER

A spider, displaced by accident
– my mower caught his web –
returns on foot, approaching the house,
manfully plodding down the path.
He looks like a grandfather, coming to say
forgive, forget, he's perfectly willing
to try again, but first, by God,
first, he'll have my apology!

IN THE ARCHIVES

Only in photographs – going, gone –
never again on the Serengeti,
the ostrich, lemur, snub-nosed langur.
Not to be seen on this earth again
Kashmir stag and tamaraw,
blackfooted ferret, spectacled bear.
Lost in the archives, nowhere at all,
the cheetah's face, intensely small.

ANT

So strange, before I'd paused for thought
I struck him dead, this common ant,
a porter who'd crossed my line of sight
bearing a plume: white pillow-feather.
Unadorned, he'd have gotten by
as the farmers did down the terraces,
setting out rice shoots, bent to the work,
under one Commissar or another.

GOATFISH

You have no ears to hear a name,
miniature mullet with tufted barbel,
bottom-dweller, using your beard
to stir up food, eating anyoldthing
in your goatly way. You couldn't care less
what we call you, simply intent to persist
as who you are, as who you are,
goatfish

What you do is continue, loving
Pooh and the *Four Quartets* and every
blooming boy or girl you see, all
total men, all full-scale
women under full-sail.
I myself have a problem, namely
me . . . but you are absolutely
you.

A Father

Still in boyhood's sleep when he died,
I gathered scraps of evidence,
made him up from memories
of his clopping me when I passed too close,
his bawdy laugh with a waitress once,
the naps he took in trousers and undershirt,
angers in the kitchen, joyously
slammed-down pinochle cards with friends . . .

from his Yiddish jokes, from the orange-striped robe
he wore down Trenton Avenue
when we walked to the beach where I sat alone
squinting in slat-lined light beneath
the Boardwalk. Forty years it took
before I'd admit the hand that clopped me
wasn't sending a Yiddish joke
but a casual, lethal communication.

Who was this father, and what was I,
only a target, a scuttling backside?
Once on a plane to Kentucky I gazed
in the eyes of a little child, a girl
named Jadell, five months old, said her mother,
window-seated, the child between us.
I gazed and saw such completeness there
she made me a while complete.

Did he ever see me so perfect, my father,
all drowsing or noise? Did he laugh when I grabbed
a finger?
Some days it's like me who died,
from his unlit eyes,
from his face turned away.

I've known the weariness of entrapment,
sagging hopes, male misery;

I can imagine a hopelessness
so deep a child
only brings more pain;
and yet all these years of wanting warmth
from him, entitlement to being! –
warmth from eyes now empty sockets;
a smile from a face so long underground
it's simply a mask of bone.

A Healing

for Michael Cuddihy

In a vision I stood by an old Apache,
heavily turning his spindle for him,
keeping him alive, I thought,
the yellowy thread of wool down the stick
dangerously thinning and yet not breaking
until he motioned to turn it himself,
for once in his faltering hands it jittered,
slowed, stopped, the last of the wool
adhering. And then it began to glow
a golden green, like a reed in sunlight,
become a delicate, folded grass
he cut, and with a taper lit
my half, then his, to sun-gold light
whose smoke was air. I felt great ease.
How can I tell you in words that ease?
Think at last of an easing heart
that slows to a steady pace after years
of running, pulsing out *win, win, win*.
Stunned by that massive sense of ease
which meant I too had taken on
my life and death; with no need to speak;
with a smile that both of us shared like the glow
of daylight, we settled side by side,
side by side, smoking together.

Some Performers

PROFESSORS

You know Professors they talk and they listen
to how they talk and to how they listen
except for some few some very few who
listen to how you talk and to how you
listen

DANCERS

They stamp their feet and swirl like trees
becoming wind becoming dust
upon that wind they yearn they grow
so twistingly they suffer now
they leap they soar they disappear

LINES FOR A SHAKUHATCHI FLUTE

House emerge house emerge from darkness
mist behushed all mist behushed all morn
snail-thought sly-force air-above-an-island
hear my call oh hear oh hear my call

TRANSLATED FROM BASHŌ

Cicada mere shell
its substance become all voice
it sang out so hard

Part Two

Open House

To somehow become invisible,

or to soften the borders toward absence enough
so that people who love you would never know
if they'd left Liechtenstein for Belgium:
pure welcome!

So there's an ambition: not to be there,
not stand in your way, letting anywhere
occur, doors open, the untutored wind
at large in a house without edges.

Living Lightly: A Blessing for Franklin Lee

1.

Ah, la, sing it, Franklin —
ready or not, here you come!
Sweet fellow with such eyes, you talk
as if your dream of Paris could be
Paris.

2.

You stroll the tide-strewn beach, you live
so lightly in this world, so calm,
a passing bird
might pause for rest
on your shoulder.

3.

Lightly, like Ariel, do it, Franklin;
absence is over, you come alive
and strangers stop to give advice
and parking places open up
and even waiters love you.

4.

You are a Prince with seven friends.
You are the dog that would not point.
You are the curving statue's light.
You are the very slowness
of your smile.

In Memory of Ed Sissman

I keep his UNICEF
Christmas card,
a collograph,
pitted footprints –
"Winter Walk,"
all in white –
with trees embossed,
stands of birch
and a riverlike stripe
in the foreground, royal
blue; and toward the top a man
in royal blue diminishing,
bound for the edge
of the scene and likely
to reach it soon, walking alone
through the whiteness – not much
more that one
can tell: he wears
a hat, a coat,
his figure is seen
strolling – somehow
you know it must
be morning, somehow
you know he's moving slowly, looking
at everything.

Dream Poem

I recited a poem in my dream, using
Morgan Freeman's slowest accent,
reading words from an elegant jar
of jam-like honey I turned in my hands.

Certain lines I repeated, as if
to demonstrate how the poem should go
in the stately voice of Morgan Freeman,
a voice I have no right to, once awake.

Slow, slow, slow down – we're here
to stay, said Robert Thurman, Buddhist
scholar, in a footnote
to this dream. We keep returning, no exit

even through death – we're here to stay
since we simply bop back, he said, as something
or other, more-or-less here forever, so
maybe we'd better think to make it

better? Smiling I turned the jar.
These are the words from my dream that survived
my waking, lines I was given to keep
sweetened by Morgan Freeman's sound:

You're not going anywhere;
You're not going anywhere;
Spoon
In alfalfa honey.

Final Page

As worldly Sappho cleanly notes,
the gods seem cowed by fear of death.
Intense as they are for experience
not one cares to learn what it is to die.

Impossibly nailed to one body cross
each life seems endless, a run-on sentence,
a wide bed meant to be garlanded
with fruit tree blossoms all summer long.

You imagine your story's final page:
blank . . . yet there you are, its reader.
What keeps you present, refusing to cease
as you think the absolute absence of thought?

The evening wind makes wild fields sigh . . .
the hills flow waterfalls of grass:
a promise of rain, to wash all clean;
the future as an answered thirst.

Ravished by notions of comfort and grace
I barely recall my name in Egyptian:
those grim-eyed hawks, those stiff figures dragging
funeral stone.

Rare Word in a Poem by Kenneth Rexroth

The curious anastomosis of the webs of thought.

FROM "AUGUST 22, 1939"

Twelve years after the brute-making deaths
of Sacco and Vanzetti, the poet
Rexroth used the handsome inkhorn
term *anastomosis* among
other words of angered despair
over those who out of greed and fear
would throw down, wall in, kill, pervert
the beautiful force
of intelligent life.

The word means "to give mouth": to what
had been stopped till then at a broken place,
or as streams ramify, or the baffled blood
invents original channels, or after
even horrors paths appear.
What is it for, asks the poem, this labor
of poetry? As you knew well,
Kenneth, dour unceaseable man,
to open passage: find a way: give mouth.

Message to the Widower

In an envelope in a favorite book
she left him her final message: a lock

of her hair . . . and with it the thought that she knew
surely one day he would find it there

and how he would feel,
finding it there.

Gates

Blocking my path through broad, flat country,
no wall or fence to either side,
stands a rusting gate . . . still locked. Were the gateposts
sunk too deep for rooting out?

Another useless gate . . . I simply
walk around, the silly lock
a joke I slowly understand

who once would have prayed to the undeniable
fence or wall that somehow I'd find

its gate's secret key in my hand.

Maple Tree

Tree, you Old Man of the Tribe
yielding the neighbors intricate shade,
in autumn burning to the bone,
through winter elegantly brave

and then in bud again a bride,
all spring a Daphne to fall in love with,
in full leaf bearing my father's essence,
his great sad face intensely calm —

whatever person you are, my tree,
immense in summer before the house,
we balance pain: I who have left . . .
you who can never come after.

In Chekhov

In Chekhov, no matter what horrors occur,
people keep saying things to each other.
Some breathless Masha, August wind,
some Nina, Donya, scent of sunned linen,
continues to speak, although she's chosen
a dreadful trade at last: the clothes
of the dead, coachman's boots and jerkins,
haggling rubles with widows and orphans,
talking, talking, on and on.
Chekhov's dying words: "So long
since I've had a glass of champagne!"

Travelers' Advisory

I never mind a winding road —
a road, at least, is never lost —
yet think of the twists in the devious way
to the City of Z from the City of A.

In the City of Z all's so orderly!
The bed's for sleeping, not for despair,
not for extremities of care,
caution and clothes thrown everywhere.

A strange long trip it's been getting there
to the City of Z . . . but would you dare,
if you had the choice, return to replay
the terrible games of the City of A?

I've heard the mystic teachers say —
gazing about in warm-eyed pity —
that A is Z, and Z is A,
whatever the journey, its all one City . . .

perhaps . . . but roads run ceaselessly
and the rule of the road is you cannot stay,
whatever your dread in the City of Z . . .
whatever your hope in the City of A.

Looking at a Lizard

My only purpose this moment
is looking at a lizard.
Does he know he's not alone?

He breathes with tiny push-ups
skin all hairline caverns
soaking up the sun.

I doubt, alive, I'm liable to get
closer to timelessness than this,
looking at a little lizard breathing.

California Poem

I'm reading my works to The State of California,
to the seals and freeways, Salinas, Santa Barbara.
I buried my Eastern thoughts at the edge of Nevada,
slipping through customs without a sigh to declare.

I'm testifying from tears over early Saroyan;
Anaheim one-liners heard on the Bob Hope Show;
girls in cling-Jantzens in 1947;
navels I sucked as a child in Camden, N.J.

For the Bay Bridge, the deserts, Eureka, Catalina;
for *Of Mice and Men* ("to live off the fat o' the land");
for the native greens, for the mad-dog waves at Carmel,
I'm reading my works to The State of California.

Inheritors

In the time of friendly ghosts, the hour of almost waking, I was given to see
my gray suit and my white suit and my hanging shirts, how they would be
after I die.
Sent to the Good Will, the Salvation Army,
they'll wait in the shops there,
the Thrift Store.
Streetmen, young actors, mothers of families
(who remember everybody's size)
will touch their shoulders, my clothes, in passing.
One stops at my drawstring pants, my brown-check sweater or my blue:
an appraising look – this might do –
a lifting off the rack.

I pity them, lonely, like dogs without masters;
sorrow at their isolation, without me to understand them
who know so well all their uses and failings,
the spot, the hole, the tendency to wrinkle,
the dashing combinations.
Listen, clothing, you will live again.
Some craggy-faced guy from Oklahoma
will fit the white suit, for seven dollars,
get a compliment from a drinking buddy
at Hobey's Country Music Bar,
crack a shy grin, tip out a Pall Mall, looking sharp,
cross-legging the crisp-creased trousers:
Yessir, feelin' *riiight!*"

And the three-piece gray
goes to a young guy with his woman friend.
"Hey, look'it this, nine bucks," he tells her.
"Try it on," she says. "Let's see the vest. Check out the trousers."
(Someday they'll pull them off, in a hurry for love;
later, thoughtful, he'll iron the creases tight, hung on a wooden hanger).

And there'll be kids to wear my blue and my brown-check sweater,
husbands tying my six ties, grandfathers in my shoes.
The underwear, of course, the underwear, too intimate, burns with the burning.
But the rest, out there, gaining new affections, passes on from me,
from my airy, smoky body
that once buttoned these cuffs,
put keys in these pockets.

Homage to Duchamp

for Teddy Macker

Thinking about his "Readymades" (corkscrew,
stool-mounted bikewheel, famous urinal)
immediately I see how my chair
from the Good Will ($12.99) is a puffy
readymade, and my papercutter,
its arm at priapic angle, White-Out-
scabs on its matte-gray grid, and likewise
the guy who honks his horn three times
at 2 AM, he's a readymade
like my cat on my lap, like I myself
and a cry of drunk laughter from Bath Street.

Uncle Sunshine

Above his father's produce store
on the East Side, on the second floor,
Uncle Solly, baby of the family,
pushed out a screen, playing with a ruler.

1908. Screen, ruler and Solly
plunged to the ground floor's rolled-up awning.
Head slammed on a framing pipe,
Sol curled in that canvas sack

till his father's noon time turning crank
creaked down ruler screen and son
slam to the sidewalk, which is the reason
my Uncle remained, throughout his life

a little dim: no Solomon
was Uncle Sunshine, Uncle Sol;
a stammer, a tendency to fall,
that was the way I knew my Uncle,

his nickname "Pep," his speech blurred,
famous for a cheery word
in the neighborhood. He'd say, "Hey, Bud,
I never see you!" every time

he saw me. He ran an elevator,
one old downtown building or other.
Remember those elevators, Biblically slow?
If I could catch their metallic smell,

linoleum floor, barrier gate
for callused hands to manipulate,
warm and tired as floors ease past:
office doors of chicken-wired glass,

rising, falling: cut-rate dentist,
violin repair, insurance place . . .
Ground – all off. End of the line.
Pep. Slow Solly. Uncle Sunshine.

Living-Space

"Imagine your ideal living-space,"
says the exercise in the writing-book.
Why not? I'll inhabit this one huge room,
large-paneled skylight, hanging plants,
workbench-clutter, paints, books,
john and kitchen. The plants look lush,
the panes of the skylight gleam, somewhere
I must have ladders and watering cans,
buckets and brushes and squeegies . . . and servants?
– to water the plants, to polish the skylight . . .
but where will they live? – they'll come in daily,
commute from the suburbs, earn twice what I do . . . .

Fine. I'll sleep in the loft on a futon
enjoying the pattering rain above
(the servants need to crawl on the roof
to clean the skylight after the rain?
– but with lots of wonderful mental and dental
medical insurance, believe me,
workman's compensation . . . okay?).

I'm thinking of adding a Japanese garden,
I see the gardener already,
raking white gravel: symbolic patterns:
mountains, sea; also, he tells me
his troubles: a kid in the gangs, a brother

who wants my help in landing a filmscript,
I'm not in the filmscript business, why me?
but right, I owe him something, I brought him
in, must do what I can, of course
he can't really garden, his rheumatism:
fulltime I'm raking gravel, revising

a filmscript, standing off the gangs,
and its clear I'll need a House Social Worker,
Guards, Union Stewards, a Day-Care Center
to do this thing right, this imagining.

Part Three

The Hope of the Air

Michael, trapping a wasp in a cup,
opened the window it battered against
and tossed it free.

So each of us
unable to find our own release
at times as incomprehensibly
are thrown from the darkness
by who knows what grace
into the hope of the air.

Inventory

Snail slime . . . snail silver.

Morning-glory-one-eyed climber.

Abandoned statue's shoulder dust.

Obsessive ant, collecting goods.

Age-lines sketched in an infant's palm,

crazy monkey under the skin . . .

and flowers, so brave you could mother them:

their innocence! they have no clothes

and follow wherever the brilliance goes.

Italian Restaurant

"You look," she teased, "like an Italian restaurant!"
"I do? You mean my massive menu,
my flickering neon sign . . . my glad-handing
maitre d' . . . ?"

"Your checkered shirt!"

But later she noticed the mandolin music,
the glowing goblets of Valpolicella,
ordered the *Ziti Gran Tympani,*
flaming.

The Good Burglar

. . . the youth broke into the home and made the bed,
washed the dishes, folded the laundry, dumped the trash
and stacked the newspapers.

NEWS ITEM

"I'll clean your house," reads the burglar's note,
"for as long as you live here." He signs himself
"Prince Eddie." Eddie, your mother reveals
you're twelve, "mentally disabled,"
your "victim's" unwatered flowers caught
your eye. In Gilroy, California,
the well-named head of police, Vern Gardener,
"doesn't want to pursue" the case,
but listen, Eddie, please, I do:
if you're "disabled," innocent Prince,
then what are we? "Abled"? Unlikely.
I love in your note where you say "Don't worry,"
your father's "a Duke in Spain," you won't
take anything, just care of the poor slob's
needy life and dry flowers forever –
Prince Eddie the burglar, breaking in!

A Gist

Until he died my father managed
a produce market in Camden, N.J.,
City Hall across the way
and two blocks farther down the "Y"
where he went to nap at 4 each day
because he woke at 4 a.m.
to do the buying on Dock Street in Philly:
potatoes, spinach, oranges — the Market
closed at six with the clang of a bell.

One Saturday when I was nine
he settled me down to work with a bushel
of lima beans, each rotting hull
smearing black on my fingers, ugly . . .
yet out of this slime came delicate green:
beans, young jade, a new-born-green.
I dropped them into a half-pint box
of wood so frail you could see the light
through amber, almost-paper sides.

I filled the box, and saw them sold,
my innocent beans, to a bargain-hunting
loud old Grandma of Families
who could have been the Queen of Death
so musty black her clothes, with hairs
on her chin . . . this Spirit Guardian
of rotting pods, she smiled at me
and the little ones that I'd set free
in their light-filled box, transformed.

Living Alone

1.

Living alone, I've gone quietly crazy,
gazing at snow on laden branches,
day after day distinguished as snowflakes.

A carton of milk will threaten to sour:
I'll stand there at the kitchen counter
drinking against the thought of waste,

filling and filling the white-streaked glass.

2.

Sleeping hard, mouth open, I dreamed
my sighs were so sweet a hummingbird entered
to feed on my breath, to lodge in my chest.

I can't cough it out, its wings so swift
I vibrate as I come awake
and all down the day every day I'm humming,

drawn toward the languishments of night.

3.

I still see the stranger who once sat beside me,
only two windows between, as her train
ran wheel to wheel a while with mine.

We both stared politely ahead till our tracks
slowly swerved apart: then we turned at last,
smiled, face to face, laughed, threw a kiss,

waving goodbye, flooding with trust.

4.

A gentle May evening . . . no place to go . . .
at the root of my being hard time to do,
heavy sugars to pull up the stem.

My sister Silence brushes my hand
and I think how they claim that the hair of the dead,
unnotified, continues to grow.

A moth beats the windowscreen, wanting in.

Draped Elegance

Draped Bentley, 1992

A PHOTOGRAPH BY JANE GOTTLIEB

A color photograph of a draped Bentley
(the title claims a Bentley's under there,
"icon of worship in gold-lamé").

Did the photographer supply the draping, to express
the value of the machine,
its elegance?

(surely a Bentley deserves no less)
or more likely the owner who'd insist
on the foils of the drape? We're left to guess,

at this and other purposes,
at essence dark or goldenly concealed
on our conundrum of an earth.

I think of Frost,
that we dance in a ring and suppose
"But the Secret sits in the middle and knows."

Oh, this once let's trust the sutra, shall we?
The title says that it's a Bentley . . .
that underneath there lies a Bentley.

A Death in Trinity County

Fred with his Baghdad accent would sell me
milk, gingersnaps, when I walked down to pick up
the mail – words, bills from the world – only look:
today there's a posted sign to tell me

there'd been a highway accident – Fred
did not survive. "We love you Fred" –
that's what the scrawl of the market sign said,
plus "Closed," like Fred's life, in a second rid

of whatever he'd prayed for, whatever he had –
a reach for a cigarette lighter, his eyes
off the road – that's the theory – and swerving he dies
in the Trinity River – his steering wheel did

him in, it crushed him at the neck.
The volunteer firemen managed to hack
him out, but who'll bring him breathing back
to the Ponderosa Market? The wreck

belongs to the junkheap now, and death
gets smiling, chatting Fred, who'd tease
the children who finger out pennies for candies,
who take for granted out-breath . . . in-breath . . . .

The Practice

The practice of the dogs is to bark,
to love their friends, sniff, frisk about;

and of the wind to change its mind,
huff and puff,
blow the house down;

and of muscles to lift;
and of hair to stir the heart;

and of my cat to blink,
to wash herself, to sleep.

And the practice of clouds
is rain; of the mountains . . . valleys;

of continents . . . new seas;
and of the days . . . the days.

Free Thursday

Free Thursday at the Art Museum
you stand so long before a painting
of four tipsy monks on a bridge in a gorge

that when this homeless fellow comes close
to hit you up for some change you whisper
"How much?" "What?" "How much do you want?"

This stops him. He tilts his head like a bird . . .
you're either nuts or a pervert . . . he starts
to slide away. Then stops. Whispers:

"How much you got?" – and you want to give him
everything: your three credit cards,
impeccable credit rating, job,

Volvo, laptop, gift of gab.
In shame you slip him a dollar. He nods.
Outside the kids are climbing the statues;

outside it's happening: play of the fountain:
wind snapping ten-foot banners: birds
cheeping in trees like cascading pennies.

Squirrel Cage

All my life I've kept bucking, like you,
for A's: respect: money: spinning
my squirrel cage, committed Samson
grinding a one-man-tribe's hard grain,
lashed to the millwheel, know what I mean?
And if I slowed, disheartened, say,
the din of five billion other wheels
oiled or squealing would get me going
at speed again. Some teachers claim
if all of us ceased, for an instant, an instant,
our self-made wheels would disappear,
we'd fully inherit who we are,
and all we'd need would be spoon and bowl,
maybe a hat for the rain, a roof
for snow, a car a child a love
and we're spinning as fast as before, familiar
churn and hum of the squirrel cage,
scurrying, hear what I'm saying? – sometimes
even helping a neighbor to turn
a stalled, a stubborn wheel.

Songs for the Downright Poet

1.

From an ancient Chinese treatise on drawing
The Downright Poet learns to treat trees

as if they held still
so birds might land;

that it's best to think of the falling rain
as God's hair;

that a stone has seven sides
but only one allows itself

to be drawn; that dark or light, of course,
may always be rendered from any direction.

2.

Late summer: the sound of a passing plane . . .
alone, unsure, beyond praise or blame,
he ponders the phrase "there is no problem"
and sits to his work of breathing well,
mindless warmth on back and shoulders.

3.

The Downright Poet discovered by chance
the recipe for *Black Ambrosia:*

"Take almonds, date-bits, raisins: slowly
mix in your very most beautiful bowl
with chocolate sauce and honey and eat
as frequently as possible."

4.

To study the absolute need to dream,
scientists set a cat on a brick
in water: how long could it hold off the drift
into sleep? The D.P. feels as drenched
as that drifting cat. He's not holding off.
He's an Astronaut, far, far from home,
sinking into the dust of the moon.

5.

The Downright Poet jogs by the sea
without a house in sight. He sets
one foot after the other, passing,
passing, bound to keep moving. The moon,
from long habit keeps bringing the new tides in.

When the sea is tranced in unearthly calm
he'll set out to cross its watery fields,
jog down its vastness day and night
the far verge always receding until

he senses a line against the horizon,
off in the distance the headlands of darkness,
the other, opposite, shadowy shore.

Campers in the Tide

No use to tell them to move inland,
these campers in the tide; their theme
is loss, they choose their inundations,
lifelong comings of tonnage of water
destroying the day. They'd scorn a seawall,
a cliff foundation above disaster.
They're waiting for us to cherish them
for who they are, each suffering thing;
to hold them in their helplessness;
cup them in our hands, all care,
ashamed of the merest flinching.

The Catch

in memory of James Wright

His words make the heart shiver
as when dawn
invades the darkness, or dusk
the light.

He could sense, in a turtle
– neck-stretched, hopeful –
all the sadness
and hunger of life.

Say he was out there
seeing it
a long time coming,
his going . . .

his insouciance
beautiful to watch –
easy glance over shoulder
moving toward the wall,

toward the miraculous
catch
in the pounded leather glove
in far left field.

The Other

Freud reports feeling an instant distaste
for the man who entered his train compartment
suddenly there, very old and ugly,
invading the doctor's private quarters,
he with much work to do, who suffered
no fool or interruption gladly.

And then, uncanny, plunge of the mind as he
sees its himself – horror! – two Freuds
in one small compartment, one clearly crazed,
his wild-eyed idiot-döppelganger
glaring . . . from the mirror-backed door
that, swinging in, had doubled him:

relief, a joke, the rational
restored. And yet . . . once teased, who'd ever
forget that ugly old man again,
that Other, who any second now
may enter, take over? one's very ghost
arriving before its time.

Fourteen

Imagine a bullet-ball, looping it hot
to your second baseman who twirls to hit
the prehensile stretch of the first baseman's mitt:
it's that famous double-play as announced
on radio by lilting Bill Stern:
" . . . smash to the infield, the Kid is there,
to Evers, to Chance, three up three down,
take it away, Red Barber!" – music
of childhood, clerking produce in Camden,
my bedroom hung with pennants: the A's,
the Phillies, loving them both and my uncle
who came to run the family store
when my father, as they say, *passed away,*
passed on, at rest: Uncle Sammy,
who brushed the fuzz from the peaches, set
bushels of kale in the entryway.
Gambler, drinker, he gave me ice skates,
boxing gloves, bought me one day
the first glass of beer of my life, so cool,
me they already called 'the Professor'
standing proud beside my uncle,
fourteen years old, in white coat and apron,
among the men at the noontide bar.

Whitewater Vision

Like everyone else I've served my time
lying under the weight of a mountain,
breathing stones . . . yet always my blood,
like leveling water, knows where it's wanted.

∽

Once I had a whitewater vision:
beneath the rage of the rapids I sensed
the undersound to the river's sound . . .
indistinguishable from silence.

∽

Who am I? Not a solving . . . a seeing.
I'd view the storm through eyes of calm.
I'd speak to say
where the silence is.

∽

On days when it seems the food for the journey
is clay, not bread, and the spirit famished,
as dusk transfigures everything
I pause, near silence: listening.

What Breathes Us

Regards to the day, the great long day
that can't be hoarded, good or ill.

What breathes us likely means us well.

We rise up from an earthly root
to seek the blossom of the heart.

What breathes us likely means us well.

We are a voice impelled to tell
where the joining of sound and silence is.

We are the tides, and their witnesses.

What breathes us likely means us well.

Part Four

The Sandwich

Remember that outrageous sandwich
you ordered from the deli menu?
How impatiently you waited,
sipping more water than you wanted,
rearranging the silverware,
before your first huge shameless bite?

But then came conversation
about some triumph that you yearned for badly
so you'd be rich and famous and the eater
of just such sandwich as you hardly noticed
dissolving through the rapid genuflections
of your ardent mouth.

Sad the glory's lessening:
last crisp click of bacon, final
turkey succulence; the tiny smile
of tomato in the small embrace
of bread so fresh, so
sourdough —

which made you stop to think a bit,
for where had you been while all the rest went down?
Oh, now you study even every
pepper grain, each remnant trace
of mayonnaise . . .
going at it
slow.

Reading an Old Friend's Poems

An evening with his new book,
scent of its paper
like linen for the first time worn,
his reverence for loveliness
comes over me
like air before rain – remember – ?
that freshness: cool, delicate . . .
though air so offered will lift at times
into a wind, a sting of sand
in the deluge that follows.
So the sweetness of this voice
in its sayings of loss
leaves taste of blood on the teeth, tart taste
that can't be spit out or swallowed.
"Where will we go,"
asks one poem at the last,
"when they send us away from here?" –
the body gone
with all its familiar devisings
and gone the mind that savored well
its unyielding will
to continue.

Reading Rilke

Things, their muteness, how they seem
to need us. "Are we only here
for saying House, Bridge, Fountain . . . ?"

You smile, asleep, but once awake
will you offer that elemental care?

Myself, I take off shoes and stockings
reading, mothering innocence,
caressing these feet that seldom betray me.

Simplified, a thing, I return
to childhood trust, familiar world:

basement shop for buying bread;
newspaper's victories and woes;
the long, discoursing walks to school

and all assumed, the dear possessions –
the Road, and the Sea; the Music; the Doorway.

Two Takes on Roses

Rose-tops fill a crystal bowl:
in a cluster of roses gathered up,
an outbreak of roses and yet contained,
what would it be to be one of them,
amid ease-weight of petals every bloom
among other blooms an offering,
an increase through kinship in crystal held,
at peace in an interchange of rose?

A physiologist tells us that women
sense all scents better than men, except
for roses . . . the men do equally well
with roses, so maybe there is some hope
after all.

Half-Inch

. . . the poor sons-a-bitches.

FAULKNER

Some Whitecoats tried an experiment,
fitted tiny glasses to chickens
which cast all they saw a half-inch off
so grain by grain as corn was offered
those chickens pecked where it seemed to be
where nothing was; they pecked and pecked
unchangeably unto death, forever
one half-inch from the corn.

Floaters

I might have learned to prosper with a father,
a man whose hands spread out below
the shoulder-blades and rump, who'll croon
that water does the work, that salt
is sure to buoy a body up,
relax, relax. I swim and dive
as flailing taught me to, and I
am baffled
by the floaters
in this ocean.

Saying No

for Tom Cole

It's come to me at last: there's joy
in saying no, pure no, that's how
women maintain their serious air

though their heels tilt them up on tiptoe, murmuring
"Look, it's gotta be no, sorry . . .
hold on, give us a mo . . . no . . . ."

There's also the guy who tends the roses,
Ph.D. in Astro-something,
could be big and yet he chooses . . .

or think of the boy who's silent for hours,
grinding his pistons, slow as oil
while the world cracks along with its wail and woe:

he says no, he says no
as his girl looks on
sullen amid the tools.

Birthday Verses

Each decade I wrote them, my birthday verses,
for twenty the darkest, at thirty wry,
the words for forty drenched with yearning,
fifty welcoming strangeness, change,
as if a god might enter the door . . .

and then no more, though life had eased,
worthy at last of celebration.

From sixty on I let the words go,
lived hour to hour, day by day,
as syrup in slow heavy drops drains away
from each snow-isle'd sugar maple tree.

Zen Pace

for Mark Saunders

Wincing at waste, write pocket-notes
on the innocent sides of used pages, save
long distance calls till Sunday, chase
the last slipping rice-grain around your plate
and even hurry slowly, acting
always with trustful slowness within,
mourning even the loss of a friend
with that dignity in her spirit never
gone . . . you have no need but to move,
sleep to waking, insult to love,
happening to happening
at the pace of a gradual smile, at the pace
of the hammer-stroke heart
that proceeds to the next
full beat, and then the next.

We Tartars

In Karakul hats and embroidered shirts
we Tartars are bodypersons, riding
our horses along the Steppes – we look
like Tartars, and we smell and taste
like Tartars; when we mate we mate
with Tartars in the Tartar night
from which come baby Tartars, bounced
on a knee, grabbing mustaches; such
is our way – we're Tartars, everyday.

If the good little God in His cleverness
had wanted trees instead of us,
or Englishmen, who could have stayed
His hand?

Intersection

How not to turn from the sagging man
in tennis shoes, between sister and wife,
barely able to mount the curb

to smile instead at the watchful face
of the girl whose lover dodges cars,
arms high with dripping iced cream cones?

Patch of Moonlight

Haiku/senryu

seeing her off
only incense greets him
coming back into the room

stretched on the floor
after a long day's talking
rubbing noses with his cat

first frost whitens grasses,
first white smoke
from his neighbor's cabin

snow at night:
deep-sleeping population
comes drifting down

friend not seen for years:
gray whiskers
around the boyish smile

after the staid snowfalls
the rain now
splashy as children

on and on
reading a friend's new novel
wishing to be more kind

the great dead mallow
ready for chopping
springs purple flowers

mind wandering,
suddenly driving very fast:
Mozart in the car

farmers' market
carrying flowers carefully
down crowded aisles

girls jump rope
in out pepper pepper
old man wipes his brow

evening tea
contemplating the great kindness
of everyone

before they risk a word
the poets at the lily pond
drink three cups of wine

awkward moment:
gazing into each other's eyes
a bit too long

summer's offering
ants on the windowsill
ants in the cat's dish

on Hendry's Beach
respectable, leashed dog, sniffed
by free-ranging others

collecting beach stones
holes and odd edges:
slow artistry

house-mice scurry
awake from their naps
after the heat of the day

digging out the dandelions;
readying ground
for the next generation

throw-aways at the curb:
inside-out umbrella
bed that wouldn't work

the poppies sway
the wind looks around
the cat licks herself

awake, listening:
laughter of guest love-makers
trying to be more quiet

cooling evening breeze:
the potted plants take water
yield back earth-scent

late for work
he stands there reading
an old love letter

patch of moonlight
rocking, rocking,
won't come in with the tide

Part Five

Gesture of Air

All these years I've been passing as human,
scribbling words on the margins of books
like bruises on a sleeping friend,

till now in summer the coolest wind
free of the killing dust of waste
enters my room, and my thought is cleansed:

a gesture of air: brash; child-faced.

The Wordless Body

Truth of the donkey: hunger; road;
driver's whip; heavy load . . .

and we? we're who we pretend to be:
stone partner . . . slick hunter . . . hot missionary —

creatures whose hunger never ceases,
hands and minds on forbidden places,

forever in need of a thirst to nourish,
a fur to smooth . . . a glance to cherish . . .

while all our lives sure-footedly
the body clip-clips on, sweet donkey;

the innocent body, finely wise;
the wordless body, that never lies.

The Plant and the Coal

"How can you bear," asked the young green plant,
"the earth so heavy all over you?"

"I know how you feel," said the buried coal,
"swaying lightly there in the light and air . . .
but the weight of the earth intensifies —
give dark its due. I've been millions like you,
compacted of millions of young green lives,
and when through breath again I rise
how beautifully our nature plays
in the blue flesh of the fire's thick blaze.
I am the way we end our days,
bluely returning the light you eat,
yielding the pith of your green, green heat."

Marching to L.A.

for Liz Libbey

I sat on a Berkeley bus bench reading
Czeslaw Milosz in the April sunshine.
A hurrying man enquired the hour.
"Not sure," I tell him. "Two or three."
He laughs: "Like the South. Either Tuesday or Wednesday . . . ."

(We know the South's always Monday or Sunday).

Here, it's San Francisco Ballet
plus snipers working the coastal highway
and seven teenagers, blind, who pass us
each with a hand to the next one's shoulder

(their guide, in his Christian Union jacket,
amid their chatty darkness looks somber).

They tell us their plan: to prove their worth
they're marching to L.A.; and we,
who have no plan to prove our worth,
encourage theirs – what can I say?

It's California, every day.

Some Trees

WALNUT

Each fall this tree
one week to the next
like a clicked-off light
goes dull of color

as if it were a wearied lover
who'd done something quite lovely
and will again quite lovely
come next Spring.

MIMOSA

It waits till June for blossoming
until the warmth of summer's sure.

Just so your thoughtful body waits
before it turns at last toward mine.

GINGKO

Only a Gingko knows the moment
for massively dropping its spatulate leaves,
all systems down, every sister tree
totally bare at once on that day
like a country that dies in its sleep.

LOCUST

Our volunteer locust-sprout, so gawky,
frail, we almost weeded it up,
has grown so lush it shields the house . . .

like the son you thought would never make good
returning in his cash-filled Caddie:
"Dad, Mom, See?!"

PINES

They had to root in a traveled path,
uphill, where sometimes I gun my van.

Before they think to thicken tall
I'll have to ax them out of the roadway,

these five pine seedlings, settled blind
rising where they cannot stay.

Namelessness

Clouds, fat uncles, ride the day
as I pass among pines down Dutch Creek Road
to fetch the mail from the old P.O.
when suddenly

words begin to fade . . .

weight and trap of thought-grids lift
in a light wind of the mind

and I may be seeing
as a cat or weasel sees:

direction without roadsign,

road no longer known as "road"
where these I once called "legs"
keep moving me along

through namelessness . . .
some of it gentle,
some threatening,

and some – like sky and bridge and riverbank –
even seeming to hold still

for one who walks this way, for one who will
eat words again, see reason and agree

that somehow they "are" me

or someone they'll pretend again to be.

Mela

Mela, mela, how it pleases,
Greek for "honey" – word so small
you can write it in the cold hard sand
in the time between two waves.

Poet at Bedtime

Stretching at bedtime, old body still there . . .

wind flutes the chimney, rattles the windowpane.

Dear events of a calming mind:

how did I enter this iris garden?
who is this little boy, smiling?

And again two favorite, homeless lines:
"Making honest women of my wants . . . ."
"Content, in the earth, like potatoes."

A Peacock

I preach to myself on Red Hill Road
that I've had it all, all I could hope for:

the older and the younger Cambridge;
Paris . . . playing Hemingway;

mist on the mountains, blue-brilliant sky,

and just at the edge of a treeful hollow
a wonder: a fossil toe-print, one —

where some rare dancer
touched brilliantly down?

Below the Shrine House, courting his hen,
a peacock struts, flurries his fan
with its quivering purple eyes. The world

couldn't be more astonishing
if he were spitting gems.

Lama Sayings

Budding . . . fullness . . . end.

Can you tame a cloud?

☞

We steep, making human tea.

Know this by thought alone
your teabag has yet
to enter the cup.

☞

For strivers . . . for those with great appetite . . .
let it settle.

☞

Let it settle. Let it settle.
Water's still water, no matter the mud mixed in.

Sun's still there,
whatever the weather's been doing.

☞

Pride: a cup turned over.

Distraction: a cup with a crack.

Negativity: poison in the cup.

Our original cup?

Not so easy.

Out of the sleep of our confusion:

a dream, that happens.

We're always either churning butter
or else the milk is going sour.

Sometimes, not always, there's gravy
with the potatoes.

The Solution

The handsome day fades yet still I keep studying price-tags.
How to outwit the greed that's been robbing my life?
how weary the occupying army within me
till it casts down its weapons at last with one grand clatter?

It's the fence, it's the pole and the chain that make a dog bark;
cut him free and he'll run to become the whole of the darkness.
I'll clear out this place, so whatever's voracious that enters
will stand there amazed, a thief in an empty house.

Position Paper

We'd all be known by our loveliest needs.
Please never know me too fast, too soon.

I'm Chekhov, starving the inward slave:
feeder on fear, famished gnome.

I'm Alice, partly, and partly, God knows,
Regina Victoria, Groucho's grin . . .

hoping to turn out a fatherly man
learning to practice breathing well

(in Japanese characters: SEI, sex;
SHO, essence; SEKI, will).

Intimidant of Father and
Exhabitant of Motherland,

like everyone else a special case,
I settle to sit in the wilderness

till even the timidest creatures pass,
taking me for a natural rock.

I was a stoker, a roaring boy,
a violence somehow holding together,

becoming at last a friend to calm;
intending only excessive care.

Like fireflies in the deep nights of summer
we're glowing, glowing, to find one another.

I'll play for the dusk on my wooden flute.
I'll not disappoint this fragrance.

Dumb Bird

On the campus path a slice of bread
skims at each beak-snip, then tumbles back
as one by one like arty dancers
a scatter of blackbirds gives it a peck,

till for reasons unknown except to bird-mind
they all rise at once to swoop away
and settle as ornaments of coal
to be-Christmas a tree.

But shortly they're back at the bread again;
except there's always this skittish one,
an underdog bird who halts halfway
and never quite gets his crumb.

It would be you, little Stupidon,
I'd have to pause to brood upon.
Dumb Bird, I tell you I'm tired of this,
this "Pardon me!" this "Be my guest" —

I tell you, I'll have no more of it,
your rushing part way to the bread.
Shove in, damn you, grab your share;
o timid bird, honey, eat, eat!

Courting the Moon

Again I court the praiseworthy moon,
passion too long neglected, calling her
Highness, risking her torrents to drink
from her hands.

I leave my house to the winds.
The subtle powders blow from my palms.
Together again the moon and I
stroll the white true road to Madrid.

Favored Guest

You who once lived between pen and brazier,
angry that one must kill to eat,
you've come with me, allowed me to lift you
drowsing in my arms, to bear you
here where you share a room with light.
Leaning in doorways on longhandled hammers
the butchers assumed you would learn their trade,
not knowing that you are a favored guest
in the slow house of my words.

Acknowledgments

Various poems gathered here have previously appeared, some in earlier versions, in *Alsop Review, American Poetry Review, The Antioch Review, Art Life, Ascent, The Atlantic Monthly, Bits, The Bridge, Blue Penny Quarterly, Chelsea, Cider Press Review, Cimmaron Review, Cincinnati Poetry Review, Confrontation, The Cumberland Poetry Review, Esquire, Exquisite Corpse, The Free Cuisenart, Free Lunch, Friends Of English, Fulcrum, Galley Sail Review, Grand Street, Harvard Review, The Hudson Review, Indiana Review, Interim, Into The Teeth Of The Wind, Ironwood, In Vivo, It's A Bunny, Jacaranda Review, The Massachusetts Review, Missouri Review, Mid-American Review, Mr. Cogito, Mudfish, New Age Journal, No Exit, North Dakota Quarterly, Ontario Review, The Pacific Review, The Paterson Literary Review, Perihelion, Pif Magazine, Plainsong, Plains Poetry Journal, Poet & Critic, Poetry, Poetry Now, Poetry Northeast, Northwest Journal, Poet's Park, Riding The Meridian, Salmagundi, The Sequoia Review, Sewanee Review, Slate, Smartish Pace, Snakeskin, Solo, Southern Ocean Review, Spectrum, Spindrift, Switched-On Gutenberg, Syracuse Guide, Two-River View, Web Del Sol, Webster Review, Witness, X-Connect,* and *Yankee.*

Michigan State University Press is committed to preserving ancient forests and natural resources. We have elected to print this title on Nature's Natural, which is 90% recycled (50% post-consumer waste). As a result of our paper choice, Michigan State University Press has saved the following natural resources*:

4.8	Trees (40 feet in height)
1,400	Gallons of Water
820	Kilowatt-hours of Electricity
12	Pounds of Air Pollution

We are a member of Green Press Initiative—a nonprofit program dedicated to supporting book publishers in maximizing their use of fiber that is not sourced from ancient or endangered forests. For more information about Green Press Initiative and the use of recycled paper in book publishing, please visit *www.greenpressinitiative.org.*

*Environmental benefits were calculated based on research provided by Conservatree and Californians Against Waste.